The Surname Stoddart

Susan Morris &
Wendy Bosberry-Scott

The question of surnames, their origins, distribution and history, lies at the heart of genealogy as well as being fascinating in its own right.

In the 1980s and 1990s, long before many genealogical sources were even indexed, let alone online, our Surname Report service provided expert assessments of the origins, history and distribution of selected British surnames, using the sources available at the time.

Now, with so many more sources available, we believe that these reports retain their value as studies of individual surnames, and so we are gradually making the Debrett Surname Archive available online and in print for the first time. Some modern indexes have been consulted to refresh and update the reports.

Debrett Ancestry Research Ltd, PO Box 379,
Winchester SO23 9YQ
Tel: 01962 841904
Email: info@debrettancestry.co.uk
Website: www.debrettancestry.co.uk

CONTENTS

Overview

The use of surnames in England began in the Norman period, when surnames were not necessarily hereditary but usually a form of description. Some described the individual's trade or profession; others were nicknames; some gave the father's Christian name; others gave the individual's place of residence or origin.

Different surnames might be used in different documents, or more than one surname given in one document. Early descriptions were fairly elaborate and by the thirteenth and fourteenth centuries these were simpler, but still variable, and indeed the instability of surnames continued until well into the seventeenth century.

Although some Normans would already have had hereditary surnames on their arrival in Britain, the passing on of a surname from generation to generation only became customary in Britain gradually during the course of the thirteenth and fourteenth centuries. At the end of this period most of the population apparently had surnames.

Variations in the spelling of a family's surname continue to be found until the present century. Before this, as most people could not read or write, the parish clerk or other official would write down the name as they heard it.

There are four main groups of surnames:

> A – Local names, which describe a person by his place of residence or origin.

> B – Occupational names, which describe a person by his trade or profession.

> C – Surnames of relationship, which refer to the Christian name of the father or other important relative.

> D – Nicknames or sobriquets, coined to describe a person in terms of his appearance or character.

Many surnames have uncertain origins, but the name Stoddart is generally understood to fall into Category B.

Origins and early examples

Stoddart is one of a group of variant surnames that also includes Stoddard, Stodhart, Stothart, Stothard, Stothert, Studart, Studdard, Studdeard, Studdert and Stuttard (see below for a full list of variants found in the course of this study). The Victorian surname scholar M A Lower (1890) judged that the forms Stothard and Stothert were 'genteel innovations'.

The origins of a surname can only be determined by examining medieval examples of the name, and fortunately several examples survive in this instance. The following early examples of the surname are cited by the late P H Reaney's authoritative *Dictionary of English Surnames* (revised by R M Wilson)*:*

1195	Vlfus Stodhyrda	Cumberland Pipe Rolls
1219	Geoffrey Stodhurd	Northumberland Curia Regis Rolls
1286	John the Stodhirde	Cheshire Assizes
1332	Richard le Stodehard	Yorkshire

The very early examples from this list are probably by-names (descriptions of an individual) rather than hereditary surnames, but Richard le Stodehard of Yorkshire may have inherited his name from his father.

From this evidence there is no doubt that the original 'Stoddarts' from whom the surname derives were keepers of animals, although there is some doubt as to whether the animals in question were bovine or equine.

Just as a goatherd was one who tended goats, a *stodhyrde* or *stodhurd* was one who tended a stud (of breeding horses), or, alternatively, a herd of *stots*. The word *stot*, now obsolete, was used in Middle English for a horse. Chaucer's Reeve (c1386) sat on:

> ... a ful good stot that was al pomely grey, and highte [named] Scot

The thirteenth century poem 'The Owl and the Nightingale' refers to the 'stottes yne Þe stod' – the horses in the stud. The *Oxford English Dictionary* (*OED*) suggests that in Old English a *stot* might have been an inferior kind of horse.

In Northern English dialect, however, the *OED* tells us that a *stot* meant not a horse but a steer (young castrated bullock) or a heifer (the word was also used as an abusive term for a woman). The Towneley Mystery Plays refer to 'aythor cow or stott' and the *OED* gives several other medieval examples.

The Northern English word 'stot', meaning a steer or heifer, became widespread in Scotland, and George F Black's *Surnames of Scotland* (1946) cites as his earliest example of the name Stoddart (*etc*) the names David Stodhirde, John Studehird and William Studhirde, who were all tenants of Douglas in the barony of Buittle in 1376. The indications are that the name originated in England and moved northwards over the border. Black's next example is Sir James Stodart, who was presented to a chaplaincy in the Collegiate Church of Methven in 1516.

Distribution

The name Stoddart appears in three of the existing volumes of the English Surnames Series (which is very incomplete): Richard McKinley's *The Surnames of Sussex*; *Norfolk and Suffolk Surnames in the Middle Ages*; and *The Surnames of Lancashire* (published between 1975 and 1988). McKinley found a single example of the name as 'Stoteherd' in the Cartulary of Cleake Abbey, at Burnham Thorp, Norfolk, before 1350. In Sussex he also found that the name Stodherd appeared as a hereditary surname in and around Mayfield (south east of Crowborough) during the thirteenth century, but not anywhere else in that county. Thus, although there are early examples of the surname from the twelfth century in the north of England, the name was known in the extreme south not long after. This tends to suggest multiple origins, rather than a migration of Stotherds from north to south.

McKinley's *History of British Surnames* (1990) notes that the surname occurs before 1500 in Cheshire, Cumberland, Devon, Lancashire, Northamptonshire, Yorkshire and in Scotland. For some reason, McKinley omitted to include Sussex in this list, probably an oversight.

Thus recent scholarship has shown the name Stoddart *etc* appearing as far south as Sussex and Devon and as far north as Cumberland and Scotland in the medieval period. However, the earliest recording of the name we have found so far is still in the north of the country in Cumberland in 1195.

In H R Moulton's *Palaeography, Genealogy and Topography,* primarily a sale catalogue printed in the 1930's listing historical documents, ancient charters, leases, court rolls *etc*, there was one entry referring to Sir Nicholas Stoddart of Kent:

> **31 May 1624**
> Indenture of bargain and sale by Robert Archdale, gent, of London and Sir Nicholas Stoddard, kt, of Mottingham, co Kent to Robert Duck, gent, Lewisham, co Kent, and Ann his wife of a messuage called Elmesteed in Bromley and Mottingham co Kent Signature of grantors – 20/-

Mottingham is now part of London and is situated south of Eltham and north of Bromley. Sir Nicholas Stoddard of Mottingham was created a knight on 23 July 1603, in the Royal Garden at Whitehall before James I's Coronation. Sir Nicholas was also known by the name Stodder.

In 1890 H B Guppy published his *Homes of Family Names in Great Britain*, still the only published work on surname distribution in Britain as a whole. His work was based on printed genealogies and a survey of county directories for the 1880s, in which he looked especially at the names of farmers, reasoning that they were among the most stable groups in society.

He noted that there was a proportion of ten in ten thousand farmers who used the name Stoddard at that time in Staffordshire. He also noted that the name

Stoddart appeared south of the Forth and the Clyde, especially in Lanarkshire and Dumfriesshire in proportions of ten in ten thousand farmers. Guppy restricted his study to names which appeared in a proportion of 7:10,000 or higher.

Many of the sources available for charting surname distribution through the centuries are necessarily confined to the wealthier sectors of the population: in general, nobody wanted to know the names of the poor but the names of those with money or land were naturally of interest to the authorities. However, one source that covers the whole of the social spectrum is provided by English parish registers, the earliest of which began in 1538 following Thomas Cromwell's mandate that all parish priests should keep a weekly record of all baptisms, marriages and burials that took place in their parish. F K and S Hitching carried out a survey of a cross section of parish registers for the years 1601 and 1602 in 1910; incidences of a particular surname are noted by parish and county, although with no indication of numbers of references.

In 1601 Stoddard was found in the registers of Lambourne, Essex and Stodert was found in the registers of St Oswald, Durham City. In 1602 Stodart was found in Oswestry in Shropshire.

A useful guide to the distribution of surnames for the sixteenth, seventeenth and eighteenth centuries in England is provided by the indexes to wills proved, and administrations granted, at the Prerogative Court of (the Archbishop of) Canterbury, in London, which had superior jurisdiction over local ecclesiastical courts where wills were proved until 1858. The PCC thus provides a national index, although it is not an evenly representative one, as testators whose wills were proved in the PCC were mostly among the wealthier members of society, northern families had the alternative of using the Prerogative Court of York, and a disproportionate number of PCC users were local, from London or Middlesex.

A search of the printed indexes for the years 1558 to 1583; 1584 to 1604; 1605 to 1619; 1620 to 1629; 1653 to 1656; 1657 to 1660; 1661 to 1670; 1671 to 1675; 1676 to 1685; 1686 to 1693; 1694 to 1700; 1701 to 1749; and 1750 to 1800 found the following entries:

1558-1599

1573   Robert Stodarde cook, St Leonards Shoreditch
       Middx
1580   George Stodderd citizen and grocer of
       London (lands in Surrey and Suffolk)
1582   Simon Studdard citizen and fishmonger of
       London St Botolph Billingsgate
1583   Martin Stodderd citizen and butcher
       Christchurch within Newgate London

There were only four Stoddart *etc* entries found in the indexes during this period. All the testators were from London and all were tradesmen. Robert Stodarde was a cook, George Stodderd was a grocer, Simon Studdard was a fishmonger and Martin Stodderd was a butcher. George Stodderd had lands in Surrey and Suffolk and a note in the indexes appears to suggest that he had connections with the Essex Stoddard family of Mottingham.

The PCC was the usual court used for testators who died abroad and there is one example of that happening in this list; in 1653/4 Thomas Stoddard died 'beyond the seas'. Only three of the testators from the seventeenth century are from London; James Stoddarde (1608), William Stoddard (1612) and Amos Stoddart (1670). Thomas Stoddard Esq of Mottingham died in Wood Street Prison in London in 1686. Two possible relatives of his, Mary Stoddard or Staddard (she signed Staddard but introduced herself as Stoddard), widow of Mottingham, and William Stoddard, yeoman of Mottingham, had their wills proved in 1653 and 1661.

There are two entries for testators from the north of England, John Stoddart (1655), gentleman of Little Braithwaite in Cumberland and Thomas Stoddart or

Stoddert, a junior weaver of Biglands in Cumberland (1658). We also have a Welsh testator, our first incident of the name occurring that far west; Hugh Stodart of Carnarvon whose will was proved in 1654.

1700-1749

1700	John Stoddard, mariner, St Mary Magdalen, Bermondsey, Surrey
1703	Benjamin Stod(d)art, Pts
1705	John Studdert, London
1706	William Stoddard, Kent
1710	Robert Studdart, Middlesex
1710	William Studdart, Pts
1713	John Stoddard, Pts
1715	Thomas Stoddard, Kent
1717	William Stoddard, Pts
1720	John Stodhart, Kent
1724	Joseph Studdart, London
1725	Robert Stoddart, London
1726	John Studard, Surrey
1728	Alice Studdart, London
1731	Mary Studard, Hertfordshire
1744	Catherine Stodard/Stodherd/Studard, Middlesex
1746	Mark Studdard, Kent
1747	William Studard, Pts
1748	William Stoddart, Pts
1749	John Stoddart, Pts

In the first half of the eighteenth century we found several testators listed who died *in partibus marinus* ('beyond the seas'): Benjamin Stod(d)art (1703), William Studdart (1710), John Stoddard (1713), William Stoddard (1717), William Studard (1747), William Stoddart (1748) and John Stoddart (1749). There are two Stoddards, one Stodhart and a Studdard from Kent; a Studard from Herefordshire; one Stoddard and a Studard from Surrey;

and in London and Middlesex there was one Studdert, two Studdarts, a Stoddart, one Studdart and one woman who was known as Stodard, Stodherd and Studard.

1750-1800

1750	Dorothy Stodart, Carnarvonshire
1761	John Stoddart, Service, Surrey
1762	Mark Stoddard, Service, Pts
1763	Benjamin Stoddard, Pts/Surrey
1766	Francis Stuttard, Middlesex
1769	William Stodart, London
1772	Elizabeth Stoddard, Kent
1780	William Stoddard, Pts
1783	Henry Stodart, Newcastle upon Tyne
1783	Nicholas Stodart, mariner, North Britain
1785	Richard Stoddart, 'Caryefort', 'Monarch' Pts
1786	Elizabeth Stoddard, Middlesex
1789	William Stodhart, Middlesex
1793	George Stoddart, Middlesex
1793	Rev Charles Stoddart, Cumberland
1795	Michael Stoddard, Pembroke
1799	David Stoddart, Middlesex

At the end of the eighteenth century we find two testators from Wales: a Stodart in Carnarvonshire and a Stoddard from Pembrokeshire. There was one Stodart from Newcastle upon Tyne, a Stoddard from Kent, one Stoddart from Cumberland and one Stodart from 'North Britain' (this usually meant Scotland) who was a mariner. John Stoddart from Surrey (1761) was also a mariner and Benjamin Stoddard (1763) was a mariner of Rotherhithe in Surrey who died overseas. Representing London and Middlesex we found one Stuttard, a Stodart, three Stoddarts and a Stodhart.

11

For the nineteenth century, H B Guppy's survey has been mentioned above. Another important Victorian source is the *Return of Owners of Land* of 1873, sometimes known as the Modern Domesday Book. This source lists, county by county, every owner of an acre of land or more, with their residence (not necessarily the address of their property) and the acreage of their holding.

Return of Owners of Land

Cumberland:	Stoddart (8)
County Durham:	Stoddard (1); Stoddart (3)
Lancashire:	Stothard (1); Stothert (1)
Lincolnshire:	Stothard (7); Stothards (2)
Monmouthshire:	Stothert (1)
Nottinghamshire:	Stothard (2)
Shropshire:	Stoddart (1)
Somerset:	Stothert (1)
Staffordshire:	Stoddard (3)
Suffolk:	Stoddart (1)
Yorkshire West:	Stothard (2)

This shows a weighting towards the north of England. Cumberland had the highest number of Stoddart *etc* landowners, with Lincolnshire coming second with seven Stothard landowners. The variants Stotherd and Stothard were more in evidence in the nineteenth century; we have thus far found very few examples of the name as such.

C W Bardsley's *Dictionary of English and Welsh Surnames with Special American Instances* (1967) includes a survey of some directories from the latter half of the nineteenth century. The following entries, and numbers of occurrences, were found for Stoddart variants:

Directory for West Riding of Yorkshire 1867
Stoddart – 2

London Commercial Directory 1870
Stodart – 2
Stoddard – 1
Stoddart – 7
Stodard – 1
Studdard – 1
Stuttard – 1

Lancashire Directory 1873 (Manchester area)
Stuttard – 3
Stutard – 1

Wilson's New York Directory 1877
Stodart – 1
Stoddard – 18
Stoddart – 10
Stodard – 1

Crockford's Clerical Directory 1881-91
Studdert – 2

County directories, which listed private residents as well as commercial businesses, have been published in England since the early nineteenth century. These directories do not include every household in a given area: people paid to be included and so the poorer members of society, such as labourers, were never included and only a few craftsmen were mentioned. Likewise, not all tradesmen were covered as the commercial section of the directories tended to concentrate on the central shopping area of the town concerned, ignoring the outlying streets. Moreover, Bardsley did not consult directories in all counties of

England. This means that his survey was not comprehensive but it gives a rough idea of the distribution of the name.

In 1867 there were only two entries for the name Stoddart in the west riding of Yorkshire. In 1870 a London directory showed seven Stoddarts and a wide range of Stoddart variants. In Manchester in 1873 there were three Stuttards listed. New York had in 1877, one Stodart, eighteen Stoddards, ten Stoddarts and one Stodard. Finally, Bardsley made a survey of *Crockford's Clerical Directory*. Between 1881 and 1891 he only found two Studderts listed.

Edward MacLysaght's *The Surnames of Ireland* (1977) and *Guide to Irish Surnames* (1965) state that Studdert was: 'An Anglo-Irish name well known in Cos Limerick and Clare since 1669.' MacLysaght states that the usual form in England was Stodart and he defined the meaning of the name as 'keeper of horses'. Sir Robert Matheson in his *Special Report on Surnames in Ireland* (1909) notes that some Stoddart *etc* families also used the variant Stotherg and Stothers. Sir Robert was the Registrar General for Ireland at that time.

There was no sign of the surname in T J & Prys Morgan's *Welsh Surnames* (1985).

The first decennial census return in England, Scotland and Wales was taken in 1801, but personal information was only recorded from 1841 onwards. From 1851, the age, occupation and birthplace is given for each member of the household, and so these records provide invaluable genealogical information as well as a fascinating 'snapshot' of the family in the nineteenth century. The latest return currently open to public inspection is that of 1911 and there are now national surname indexes to the returns from 1841 onwards, although these indexes contain many misreadings. Using these indexes, we found the following numbers for Stoddart, Stoddard, Stodhart, Stothart, Stothard, Stothert, Studart, Studdard, Studdeard, Studdert and Stuttard in England, Scotland and Wales:

6 June 1841

Stoddart (1289); Stoddard (274); Stodhart (62); Stothart (157); Stothard (466); Stothert (97); Studart (17); Studdard (23); Studdeard (7); Studdert (1); Stuttard (262)

30 March 1851

Stoddart (1624); Stoddard (260); Stodhart (44); Stothart (105); Stothard (456); Stothert (75); Studart (14); Studdard (30); Studdert (1); Stuttard (370)

7 April 1861

Stoddart (1610); Stoddard (266); Stodhart (25); Stothart (126); Stothard (446); Stothert (70); Studart (35); Studdard (41); Studdeart (7); Studdert (14); Stuttard (306)

2 April 1871

Stoddart (2022); Stoddard (403); Stodhart (34); Stothart (123); Stothard (600); Stothert (115); Studart (36); Studdard (21); Studdeart (5); Studdert (7); Stuttard (540)

3 April 1881

Stoddart (2507); Stoddard (488); Stodhart (31); Stothart (175); Stothard (646); Stothert (93); Studart (32); Studdard (19); Studdeart (4); Studdert (6); Stuttard (654)

5 April 1891

Stoddart (2671); Stoddard (532); Stodhart (29); Stothart (162); Stothard (687); Stothert (109); Studart (38); Studdard (51); Studdeart (12); Studdert (24); Stuttard (662)

31 March 1901

Stoddart (3093); Stoddard (517); Stodhart (36); Stothart (183); Stothard (837); Stothert 113; Studart (27); Studdard (49); Studdeart (19); Studdert (23); Stuttard (800)

2 April 1911

Stoddart (1943); Stoddard (529); Stodhart (20); Stothart (103); Stothard (887); Stothert (125); Studart (32); Studdard (15); Studdeart (19); Studdert (22); Stuttard (929)

As can be seen, the variant Stoddart emerged from this analysis as the strongest, followed by Stothard and then Stoddard.

Famous bearers of the name

W A Shaw's *The Knights of England* (1906) lists two men of the name Stoddart *etc* who were knighted before 1906. Sir Nicholas Stoddart has already been mentioned above; the other was:

> John Stoddart LLD, president of the High Court of Appeal, and judge of the Vice-Admiralty Court at Malta - created 27 July 1826.

Moving forward a century or so, in the 1996 edition of *Debrett's People of Today* the following references were found:

> Baron Stodart of Leaston (Life Peer UK 1981)
> James Anthony Stodart PC
> Antony Leslie Stoddard - solicitor & vice president of
>   Dolphin Holdings Ltd, Dubai
> Christopher James Stoddard - surgical registrar
> Anne Elizabeth Stoddart CMG - UN representative
> Christopher West Stoddart - managing director
>   GMTV Ltd
> John Joseph Stoddart - photographer
> Professor John Little Stoddart CBE - biologist
> John Maurice Stoddart CBE - vice chancellor,
>   Sheffield Hallam University
> Sir Kenneth Maxwell Stoddart KCVO, AE, JP - retired
> Michael Craig Stoddart - chartered accountant
> Patrick Thomas Stoddart - media consultant
> Peter Laurence Bowring Stoddart - insurance broker
> Baron Stoddart of Swindon (Life Peer UK 1983)
> David Leonard Stoddart

The British *Dictionary of National Biography* has entries for the following:

> Andrew Ernest Stoddart (1863-1915) – cricketer
> Charles Stoddart (1806-1842) – diplomatist
> Sir John Stoddart (1773-1856) – journalist and judge
>   (see below)
> Thomas Tod Stoddart (1810-1880) – angler and poet
> Charles Alfred Stothard (1786-1821) – antiquarian
>   draughtsman
> Thomas Stothard (1755-1834) – painter and illustrator
> James Stodart (died 1810) – merchant and local
>   politician

Coats of Arms

There are several coats of arms listed in Burke's *General Armory* granted to men of the name Stodart, Stoddard, Stoddart and Studdert:

> **Stodart** (Kailzie co Peeble, Ormiston co Edinburgh; represented by Robert Riddle Stodart Esq, Lyon Clerk Depute) - Quarterly 1st and 4th argent a fess nebuly between three stars of six points sable a bordure gules; 2nd and 3rd argent a chevron between three bull's heads couped sable armed vert for Turnbull. Crest - A star of six points argent issuing out of a cloud sable. Motto - *Post nubes lux*.

> **Stoddard** - Sable a garb argent a border engrailed of the last

> **Stoddart** (Southhouse co Edinburgh 1672) - Argent a fess nebuly between three stars sable. Crest - A star issuing from a cloud proper. Motto - *Post nubes lux*.

> **Stoddart** (London; George Stoddart citizen of London son of William Stoddart of same gent. Visitations London 1568) Sable three estoiles argent a border of the last.

> **Stoddart** (co Northumberland, granted 1826 to Sir John Stoddart LLD President of the High Court of Appeal and Judge of the Vice-Admiralty Court Malta) Sable two chevronels between three estoiles, in the centre point a cross of eight points (a Maltese cross) all within a bordure argent. Crest - the fasces in bend dexter surmounted by a silver oar (being the official

ensign of the Vice-Admiralty Court) in bend sinister, all encircled by a wreath of oak fructed proper. Motto - *Justitiæ tenax*

Studdert - Azure the sun or, between four mullets in bend dexter, and as many crescents in bend sinister argent. Crest - A bull's head erased ermine.

Studdert (Bunratty Castle, co Clare; confirmed to Richard Studdert of Bunratty and the descendants of his great grandfather Thomas Studdert Esq of Bunratty) - Per pale azure and gules three mullets argent. Crest - a demi horse rampant sable round the body a ducal coronet or. Motto - *Refulgent in tenebris.*

Printed Genealogies

The following references have been found to printed genealogies of Stodart, Stoddard and Studdert families:

Stodart
of Kailzie and Ormiston - *Burke's Landed Gentry* 1846, 1850, 1853
of Oliver (Tweedie-Stodart) - *Burke's Landed Gentry* 1937, 1952
M F Tweedie, *The History of the Tweedie or Tweedy Family* (1902)

Stoddard
Burke's Prominent Families of the USA
J H Stoddard *A Pedigree of the Family of Stoddard* (nd)
Harleian Society i, 27
Hasted's Kent (Hundred of Blackheath, by H H Drake) 194
New England Registers v 21-42

Studdert
of Bunratty Castle - *Burke's Landed Gentry* 1838-1898
of Elm Hill - *Burke's Landed Gentry* 1858, 1863
Burke's Heraldic Visitations
J Pratt, *Pratt Family Records* (1931)
R H Studdert, *The Studdert Family* (Dublin 1960)

Note: The entry in *Burke's Landed Gentry* for the Stodart family of Kailzie and Ormiston starts '... [it is a] tradition [that] the first of the family came over with William the Conqueror, as standard-bearer to the Vicomte de Pulesdon, a noble Norman ... The name is derived from the office of standard-bearer, and was anciently written De la Standarde ...'

Genealogies in *Burke's Landed Gentry* relied upon family submissions, not research. This theory seems likely to be a genteel fabrication: the surname is not mentioned in two works on families of Norman descent: L G Pine's *They Came With The Conqueror* (1954) and Mr Avenel's *The Norman People* (1975). The Larousse French surname dictionary *Dictionnaire de Noms et Prénoms de Franc* (1951) has no entry for the name Stoddart *etc*, nor for (de) (la) Standarde.

The 1952 entry in Burke's for the Tweedie-Stodart family of Oliver was also studied. This family suggested that their Stodart line originated from one of the three Douglas tenants mentioned by Black (see page 4) as being the earliest examples of the surname in Scotland. Since the pedigree then jumps from the fourteenth century to a man living in 1643, this assumption should be treated with caution.

Summary

To conclude, the name Stoddart is an occupational name meaning 'a herder of horses or bullocks'. Throughout our research we have found many variants for this surname including: Staddard, Stod(d)ard, Stodarde, Stodderd, Stodart, Stodert, Stodhart, Stodherd, Stodhird(e), Stodhurd, Stoteherd, Stothard(s), Stothart, Stotherd, Stothert, Stothurd, Studart, Studdard, Studdert, Studeard, Stut(t)ard and Stuttherd.

Although primarily a name from the north, the surname was unusually widespread from an early date, which does raise the question of whether the movement of drovers had any influence on its propagation. It has reached as far south as Somerset and Kent and was prolific in London and Middlesex by the eighteenth century. Stoddart is an English name, which arrived in Scotland by the fourteenth century and has travelled across the Irish Sea to the counties of Limerick and Clare in Ireland, where it has been found since the middle of the seventeenth century. Throughout our research we have found that Stoddart and Stoddard are the most commonly used variants of this interesting name.

Sources Consulted

P H Reaney, *The Origins of English Surnames* (London: Routledge & Kegan Paul 1967)

P H Reaney & R M Wilson, *A Dictionary of British Surnames* (London: Oxford University Press, 3rd edition 1995)

P H Reaney, *Dictionary of British Surnames* (London: Routledge & Kegan Paul, 2nd edition 1976)

P Hanks & F Hodges, *A Dictionary of Surnames* (Oxford University Press 1988)

M A Lower, *Patronymica Brittanica* (London 1860)

C W Bardsley, *Dictionary of English and Welsh Surnames* (1901: reprinted, Baltimore: Genealogical Publishing Co. 1967)

C L'Estrange Ewen, *Guide to the Origin of British Surnames* (London: John Gifford 1938)

H B Guppy, *Homes of Family Names in Great Britain* (London 1890)

Ernest Weekley, *The Romance of Names* (London: John Murray, 2nd edition 1917)

Ernest Weekley, *Surnames* (London: John Murray 1917)

24

George F Black, *The Surnames of Scotland* (New York Public Library 1946)

Edward McLysaght, *The Surnames of Ireland* (Dublin: Irish University Press 1977)

T J & Prys Morgan, *Welsh Surnames* (Cardiff: University of Wales Press 1985)

F K & S Hitching, *References to English Surnames in 1601* (Walton on Thames: Bernau 1910)

F K & S Hitching, *References to English Surnames in 1602* (Walton on Thames: Bernau 1911)

Debrett's People of Today (Debrett's Peerage Limited 1996)

The Dictionary of National Biography: Index & Epitome (London 1906)

The Concise Dictionary of National Biography, Part II, 1901–1950, (Oxford, 1961)

Burke's Family Index (London: Burke's Peerage Limited 1976)

H R Moulton, *Palaeography, Genealogy & Topography* (1930)

Index to Prerogative Court of Canterbury Wills (The National Archives: online)

G W Marshall, *The Genealogist's Guide* (1903; reprinted, Baltimore: GPC 1973)

J B Whitmore, *A Genealogical Guide* (London 1953)

Charles Bridger, *An Index to Pedigrees* (London 1867)

Geoffrey B Barrow, *The Genealogist's Guide* (London: Research Publishing Co. 1977)

Sir Bernard Burke, *The General Armory* (London 1884)

C R Humphrey-Smith ed, *Burke's General Armory Volume II*, (Tabard Press 1973)

The Return of Owners of Land (1873)

Eilert Ekwall, *The Oxford Dictionary of English Place Names* (Oxford University Press, 4th edition, 1960)

E G Withycombe, *The Oxford Dictionary of English Christian Names* (Oxford: Clarendon Press, 2nd edition 1950)

W J Hardy & W Page, *A Calendar to the Feet of Fines for London and Middlesex: Vol 1 Richard I- Richard III (1189-1485)* (London 1892)

Richard McKinley, *The Surnames of Oxfordshire* (English Surnames Series III: Leopard's Head Press, 1977)

Richard McKinley, *The Surnames of Sussex* (English Surnames Series V: Leopard's Head Press, 1988)

Richard McKinley, *The Surnames of Lancashire* (English Surnames Series IV: Leopard's Head Press, 1981)

Richard McKinley, *Norfolk and Suffolk Surnames in the Middle Ages* (English Surnames Series II: Phillimore, 1975)

George Redmonds, *Yorkshire West Riding* (English Surnames Series I: Phillimore, 1973)

Mr Avenell, *The Norman People* (London 1874)

Debrett's Heraldry (London 1933)

J P Brooke-Little, revised, *Boutell's Heraldry* (Frederick Warne: London, 1970)

F N Robinson, *The Works of Geoffrey Chaucer* (2nd edition: OUP 1966)

Indexes to 1841-1911 Census Returns of England, Wales and Scotland (National Archives/*Ancestry.co.uk*)

B Thuresson, *Middle English Occupational Terms* (Lund, 1950)

Wm A Shaw, *The Knights of England* (2 vols, London 1906)

Dictionnaire de Noms et Prénoms de France (Larousse 1951)

Burke's Landed Gentry 1846, 1952

The Oxford English Dictionary (Oxford University Press, 2013, online)

www.ingramcontent.com/pod-product-compliance
Lightning Source LLC
Chambersburg PA
CBHW070243290526
45789CB00004B/1748